# KHUSHI'S THEORY ON TIME TRAVEL

## YES! YOU CAN ALTER YOUR PAST AND FUTURE, SEE HOW!

KHUSHI MANAN DAVE

Made with ❤ on the Notion Press Platform
www.notionpress.com

I would dedicate this to all those who are trying to find the solution to make a time machine and how is it possible. I would dedicate this to all those who are trying to find the solution to make a time machine and how is it possible. Also, most importantly, my parents.

# Contents

# Foreword

Here, I have composed this book for all the researches and questions regarding time travel, so that one can easily clarify their misunderstandings and understandings. We all are aware that we cannot travel to past and change our present, but this is actually possible, but in a rather different way then you assume it to be.

Also, in this book it is referred the way in which time travel would be possible in future.

# Preface

This book is very short, but in this it describes all about a much précising yet important theory. Here, we would get the answer regarding how time travel is possible in both future and past. Tis point came into my mind, after a prolonged thinking. So, here it shows how time travel would be done in future.

# Acknowledgements

I would like to express my profound gratitude to many people, but most importantly, my parents, Mr. Manan Dave and Mrs. Minal Dave, without whom this book might not have been writeen. Also, to a very best friend of mine, who helped me out through the process and to all my teachers.

# Prologue

This book is very short, but in this it describes all about a much précising yet important theory. Here, we would get the answer regarding how time travel is possible in both future and past.

# CHAPTER ONE

# Khushi's Theory on Time travel

Time travel, it is something that we all wonder about. Time travel is regarding the phenomena where we travel to the past or future.

So before wondering about what it is, let us first wonder about why is it so important to understand about this theory. This theory would help us discover that how time travel would occur and in which way it would. It also helps us the answer regarding the questions of Stephen Hawking, where it is assumed like "Past time travel is not possible".

In this paper there are answers to these major questions and moreover, there is also a way that how these two statements would be proven wrong and are possible. All in all, in this paper there is the answer that we can travel to the past. So, let's dive straight into it.

We are all acutely aware that according to the latest research we cannot see a way to perform time travel. But the idea regarding time travel and our general way of looking at this idea is wrong itself. Here, I have got an idea where time travel is possible, but not the way we assume it to be.

To time travel we all think that we need to create a time machine, which needs to move at very high speeds, which is not possible practically. We know that according to respected Stephen Hawking, we cannot travel to past.

But I have answer to this question. Firstly, we can never travel to future or past in our universe. Yes, because we know that we cannot travel to past (Stephen Hawking previously explained) and we cannot travel to future as well, as if for example I would travel to the future then I would go and tell my future self to do something great and once my future self would do it, and I would become very famous, my present self would stop doing it and then the things won't be the same in my future, so future travel is also not possible in our universe.

We are all aware regarding Einstein's wormhole theory and the multiverse theory. The idea is that we cannot travel in the past or future in our universe but we can surely travel to the past and future of a multiverse. We know that in the multiverses the same situation has different possibilities, and each and every possibility would turn out to be true in every individual universe of the multiverse. So, if time travel is really possible, then we would never be able to do it in our universe, rather we would be travelling to the future and past of a multiverse or another universe and doing what we want to do, and in this way the possibility that was going to be true in that universe would be taken true. Means, suppose I am giving a test and now in two universes of multiverse, the same situation has different possibilities, say in one I got fever and I didn't attend the test and in the second in I got great scores. So, in both of these universes different possibilities happened. The same goes for the time travel, say I want to be successful in the future, so I time travelled and went to another universe's future and told myself to be successful, and now I came back to my universe and relaxed thinking that I am going to be successful. So, now in the universe where I travelled I became successful and in the universe where I am right now, I didn't do much. So, in both the universe different possibilities that were going to be true did happen true, but through this way. So, in this time travel is possible.

Basically, when we would be time travelling we would be going to a multiverse, to carry out the possibility that was going to be carried out.

Now, let's pay attention to answer another question, where respected Stephen Hawking said that if time travel was possible, we would be doing it. The answer to this is that, we know that time machine is practically not possible. But, we are also aware of worm holes. So, time travel is possible through worm holes as we cannot make time machines. To make a time machine, we need to travel through $4^{th}$ dimension, which is time and inside only a $3^{rd}$ dimension object that is universe. So, to create a time machine we need to make something that helps we travel through $3^{rd}$ and $4^{th}$ dimension at the same time. So might be that we would receive a so called 'space station' or some apparent set up to receive time machines or we need to first design a time machine to receive time machines. Also might be, that inside so many universe of the multiverse, our universe is running out through a possibility where yet no time travelers have arrived and this possibility would diminish in the future. But all in all these two possibilities would only be there to be true. Let's get back to the topic-

More specifically, time travelers would also come and go through worm holes. So, since we don't know any worm hole, or say any worm hole is not near our earth or our galaxy time travelers, couldn't make it to us. Might be, in other galaxies, which we cannot see, wormhole has been discovered and time travelling is a normal act. Moreover, we can say that first we need to discover the worm hole to let the time travelers come, it's like saying that we first need mouth to eat, we don't need to eat to have a mouth. So, in future when we would discover worm hole or might be it would be created by some collision, we would be welcoming time travelers and would be going there too.

All in all, we can say that we would only get time travelers when we would start time travelling, not till that.

So, time travelling also means a tour to another universe or the past or future of another universe. And, this also means that we would only receive time travelers after we start doing the same, if there is no door, we cannot go out and neither can someone come in, so once we discover the door (wormhole), we would receive guests and we would also move out. Also, may be our universe is the one among the universes, where the possibility of worm hole not being discovered is being carried out, and it would end at some time, where the possibility of the wormhole being discovered would be carried out at that point of time, where other universes would have normalized the act of time travelling.

Also, here we can think of it as an idea where a wormhole, would help us to time travel and also travel to another universe, like we can travel from one galaxy to another.

So, a wormhole can help us travel through space-time, but also help us travel to another universe, both in one.

Basically, we can say that we would never be able to travel in past or future in our universe; also we will surely be able to travel to past, but in another universe.

All in all, the conclusion is that the statement that we could never travel to past is proven to be wrong. Also, this means that when we will discover the time machine we would also discover the machine through which we could go to another universe.

So, now let us assume how the future time travel would be like. In future, the time travel would be occurring through worm holes and if, through time machines. Also, in this we would be going to another universe.

So, here we can see how we can travel from one universe to other along with change in time.

So, here wormholes might be considered to be the tunnels in space time as well as universes.

Time machines cold also be supported by the same.

Here, I am just attaching some important points, not as a new one-

- So, time travel is possible through worm holes as we cannot make time machines. To make a time machine, we need to travel through $4^{th}$ dimension, which is time and inside only a $3^{rd}$ dimension object that is universe.
- Also, may be our universe is the one among the universes, where the possibility of worm hole not being discovered is being carried out, and it would end at some time, where the possibility of the wormhole being discovered would be carried out at that point of time, where other universes would have normalized the act of time travelling.
- "Past time travel is not possible". - is wrong
- Now, let's pay attention to answer another question, where respected Stephen Hawking said that if time travel was possible, we would be doing it. The answer to this is that, we know that time machine is practically not possible. But, we are also aware of worm holes. So, time travel is possible through worm holes as we cannot make time machines. To make a time machine, we need to travel through $4^{th}$ dimension, which is time and inside only a $3^{rd}$ dimension object that is universe.

So, now let's say you want to travel in past and alter World War-I, you can! but in another universe, where this possibility would be running. In this way time travel would be possible.

Moreover, we can say that first we need to discover the worm hole to let the time travelers come, it's like saying that we first need mouth to eat, we don't need to eat to have a mouth. So, in future when we would discover worm hole or might be it would be created by some collision, we would be welcoming time travelers and would be going there too.